A Message to Parents, Teachers, and Other Caring Adults

One of the most challenging and yet important tasks of parenting and fostering younger generations is passing on our values to children while also allowing young people, as they grow, to form their own sense of what is important. As adults influencing children, we might be tempted to follow children around, labeling for them at every turn what is important and what is not. This is futile, of course, and we would quickly become exhausted and confused trying to sort out for ourselves what is "important" versus "kind of important" or "very important." Before teaching kids what REALLY matters, we must have a fair grasp on that ourselves!

In this book, which aims to offer something to both children and adults, I propose that what REALLY matters are those things that we and others cannot live without, and those people whom we love. The end result is that each of us REALLY matters because we are loved, if not by someone close by, then by God. It is one of our human condition's saddest phenomena that some children and adults feel that they do not matter because they have suffered abuse, neglect, or other forms of human cruelty. One of the greatest ways of ensuring that your child, grandchild, student, or loved one will develop a healthy sense of what REALLY matters, is to love them and teach them to love others.

—*Br. John Mark Falkenhain, O.S.B.*

What REALLY Matters?

Something matters when it is important. Think of some of the things that are important to you: your baseball glove, your favorite game, your bicycle, or the doll your grandmother gave you.

You know something is important—that it matters—when you don't want to give it away. We tend to be extra careful with things that matter—with things that are important. We would be sad if we lost them. We would be upset if they broke.

What REALLY Matters?

A Kid's Guide to What's Really Important in Life

Written by Br. John Mark Falkenhain, O.S.B.

Illustrated by R.W. Alley

Abbey Press
St. Meinrad, IN 47577

To my nephews and niece,
Caleb, Alex, and Chloe, who REALLY matter!

Text © 2013 Br. John Mark Falkenhain, O.S.B.
Illustrations © 2013 Saint Meinrad Archabbey
Published by One Caring Place
Abbey Press
St. Meinrad, Indiana 47577

Library of Congress Catalog Number
2013934808

ISBN 978-0-87029-531-7

Printed in the United States of America.

Sometimes Things Are Important to Others

Some things might be important to other people, even if they don't matter to you. Your mother might say, "Be careful with that book. Your grandmother gave that to me when I was a little girl and it is my favorite book." That means it matters to her, even if you don't see what's so special about it.

Sometimes we accidentally hurt other people because we don't understand that something is important to them. If you accidentally ruin your brother's baseball glove by leaving it out in the rain, he will probably be very hurt and upset. You may not have done it to be mean, but you may not have been careful enough because you did not understand how important it was to him—how much it mattered to him.

What We Think Matters Can Change

As people grow up, different things become important and begin to matter more than others. When people are children, certain toys, games, and collections—like dolls or baseball cards—are important and matter a lot.

For grown-ups, cars, money, clothes, and houses can matter a lot. Grown-ups may have worked very hard for these things and so they are important, too. They matter.

How Do We Know What REALLY Matters?

Lots of things matter, but some things REALLY matter. How do we know what those things are?

One way of knowing if something REALLY matters is if we can't live without it.

Food really matters, and water really matters because we cannot live without them. That is why it is important—REALLY important—that we help those people around us who don't have enough food to eat or water to drink.

There are other things that REALLY matter that we don't always think about. For example, trees REALLY matter because they help make our air clean to breathe. And our houses and homes REALLY matter because they protect us from the rain and the cold. We could not live without either of these.

Remembering What Matters

Sometimes we forget that things like food, water, trees, and houses REALLY matter, and so we waste them or forget to take care of them.

If you have lots of food or lots of money, it can be easy to forget just how important these things are—how much they matter. But not everyone has enough. People who don't have enough money never forget how important money is, and hungry people always know that food REALLY matters.

Love Makes All the Difference

Love is another thing that makes something REALLY matter. When you love someone—he or she REALLY matters.

Your mother REALLY matters because you love her. And your father REALLY matters, even if he is away on a trip or living somewhere else for a while. Your grandmother REALLY matters, and your best friend REALLY matters because you love them.

Who are the people you love? These are the people that REALLY matter to you.

You REALLY Matter

Of course, there are people who love you. That means that you REALLY matter.

Name some of the people who love you. You are really important to them. They would be sad if you weren't around.

They love you. You REALLY matter.

You ALWAYS Matter

Sometimes people can make us feel like we don't matter. This happens when someone says something mean or does something unkind, like hurt us or ignore us for a while.

When we feel we don't REALLY matter, we usually feel sad and alone...like something forgotten.

No one should have to feel like this.

You Matter to God

But even when we feel like we don't REALLY matter—and it happens sometimes to all of us—it's just not true! There is always someone who loves you: your mother, your father, your best friend, the other adults who help take care of you.

You can also always remember that God loves you.

You REALLY matter. It is impossible for you NOT to matter!

Being Grateful

Once you know what REALLY matters, there are two things you must do. The first is to be grateful. That means saying thank you.

If you have enough food, a home to live in, and someone who loves you, then you have what REALLY matters. Remember to say thank you to your parents for all the ways they take care of you. Say thank you to your grandparents for loving you. Say thank you to God for the trees and water and your best friend—for the things that REALLY matter.

Part of being grateful is treating these things well. Take care of them. Try not to waste them.

Remember to Share

The second thing that you must do is to share the things that REALLY matter.

If you are lucky enough to have lots of food, then you can share some of it with someone who does not have enough. That way they will also have what REALLY matters.

You can also share some of your money or clothes with the poor so that they have enough to live. When you do this, you are not only giving them what REALLY matters, but you are also telling them that they REALLY matter. They may have forgotten that.

Make a List

What REALLY matters? The things we cannot live without and the people we love. Make a list of what matters. Some of the things we've already talked about are:

- ✓ Trees
- ✓ Your home
- ✓ Clean air and water
- ✓ Food
- ✓ Parents
- ✓ Grandparents
- ✓ Best friends
- ✓ Aunts and uncles
- ✓ Even brothers and sisters

✓✓ And you!

What else REALLY matters to you?

Share Your Love With Others

Each morning when you wake up, or each evening before you go to bed, think of one thing and one person that REALLY matters, and say thank you for them.

Then ask your mom or dad if they can think of someone who doesn't have what REALLY matters—food, water, a home, someone to love—and see if you can come up with a way to help them get what they need.

Being grateful and sharing REALLY matters.

One Last Thing!

Remind yourself everyday: "I REALLY matter." Then tell someone you love how important they are by saying . . .

"I love you. You REALLY matter."

Br. John Mark Falkenhain, O.S.B., is a monk of Saint Meinrad Archabbey and a licensed psychologist. His work at Saint Meinrad includes teaching and consulting in the Seminary and School of Theology, as well as doing vocations and formation work for the monastery. Br. John Mark worked with children, adolescents, and their families for several years before joining the monastery and has a particular interest in child, adolescent, and adult development.

R. W. Alley is the illustrator for the popular Abbey Press adult series of Elf-help books, as well as an illustrator and writer of children's books. He lives in Barrington, Rhode Island, with his wife, daughter, and son. See a wide variety of his works at: www.rwalley.com.